W9-ARN-193

WITHDRAWN

Pebble®

Great African-Americans

Benjamin
BANNEKER

by Isabel Martin   Consulting Editor: Gail Saunders-Smith, PhD

CAPSTONE PRESS
a capstone imprint

Pebble Books are published by Capstone Press,
1710 Roe Crest Drive, North Mankato, Minnesota 56003
www.capstonepub.com

J–B

BANNEKER

459– 6675

Library of Congress Cataloging-in-Publication Data
Martin, Isabel, 1977–
  Benjamin Banneker / by Isabel Martin.
    pages cm.—(Pebble books. Great African-Americans)
  Summary: "Simple text and photographs present the life and achievements of Benjamin Banneker,
a free African-American astronomer, author, and inventor of the 1700s"—Provided by publisher.
  Audience: Ages 5–8.
  Audience: K to grade 3.
  Includes bibliographical references and index.
  ISBN 978-1-4914-0500-0 (library binding)—ISBN 978-1-4914-0506-2 (pbk.)—
  ISBN 978-1-4914-0512-3 (ebook pdf)
  1. Banneker, Benjamin, 1731–1806—Juvenile literature. 2. Astronomers—United States—
Biography—Juvenile literature. 3. African American scientists—Biography—Juvenile literature. I. Title.
  QB36.B22M37 2015
  520.92—dc23
                                        2013049776

Editorial Credits
Nikki Bruno Clapper, editor; Terri Poburka, designer; Kelly Garvin, media researcher;
Laura Manthe, production specialist

Photo Credits
Alamy Images/North Wind Picture Library, cover, 6; Dreamstime/John Kropewnicki, 20; Getty
Images, Inc/De Agostini, 10; Glow Images/Everett Collection Stock Photos, 14, 16; Library of
Congress/Highsmith (Carol M.) Archive, 18; Photographs and Prints Division, The Schomberg
Center for Research in Black Culture, New York Public Library, Astor, Lenox and Tilden Foundation,
4, 12; Shutterstock/SYILLFX, cover art; Archives Center, National Museum of American History,
Behring Center, Smithsonian Institution, 8

Note to Parents and Teachers

The Great African-Americans set supports national curriculum standards for social studies
related to people, places, and environments. This book describes and illustrates Benjamin
Banneker. The images support early readers in understanding the text. The repetition of words
and phrases helps early readers learn new words. This book also introduces early readers to
subject-specific vocabulary words, which are defined in the Glossary section. Early readers may
need assistance to read some words and to use the Table of Contents, Glossary, Read More,
Internet Sites, Critical Thinking Using the Common Core, and Index sections of the book.

Printed in the United States of America in Stevens Point, Wisconsin.
032014   008092WZF14

Table of Contents

Meet Benjamin. 5

Early Years 7

As an Adult 11

Later in Life. 17

Glossary 22

Read More 23

Internet Sites. 23

Critical Thinking
Using the Common Core 24

Index 24

1731

born

4

Meet Benjamin

Benjamin Banneker was a famous scientist and writer. He was born in Maryland in 1731. At that time most African-Americans were slaves. But Benjamin's family was free.

*a school like the one
Benjamin went to*

1731

born

6

Early Years

Benjamin's grandmother

taught him to read.

He went to school and

helped on his family's farm.

Instead of playing,

Benjamin would often read.

a clock much like the one Benjamin built

1731
born

1753
builds a clock

In 1753, at age 22,

Benjamin built a

wooden clock. People

came from all over to

see Benjamin's clock.

It kept perfect time for

more than 50 years.

people watching a solar eclipse

1731
born

1753
builds a clock

1789
sees eclipse that he predicted

10

As an Adult

At age 57 Benjamin began to study astronomy. He read books about stars. Benjamin predicted a solar eclipse. It happened right on time in 1789.

1731
born

1753
builds a clock

1789
sees eclipse that
he predicted

12

In 1791 Benjamin helped plan Washington, D.C., the new capital of the United States. He studied the land. He helped decide where streets and buildings should go.

1791

helps plan U.S. capital

Philadelphia Aug. 30. 1791.

Sir

I thank you sincerely for your letter of the 19th instant and for the almanac it contained. no body wishes more than I do to see such proofs as you exhibit, that nature has given to our black brethren, talents equal to those of the other colours of men, & that the appearance of a want of them is owing merely to the degraded condition of their existence both in Africa & America. I can add with truth that nobody wishes more ardently to see a good system commenced for raising the condition both of their body & mind to what it ought to be, as fast as the imbecillity of their present existence, and other circumstances which cannot be neglected, will admit. I have taken the liberty of sending your almanac to Monsieur de Condorcet, Secretary of the Academy of sciences at Paris, and member of the Philanthropic society, because I considered it as a document to which your whole colour had a right for their justification against the doubts which have been entertained of them. I am with great esteem, Sir,

Your most obed. humble servt.

Th. Jefferson

Mr. Benjamin Banneker
near Ellicot's, lower mills, Baltimore count.

Thomas Jefferson's letter in response to Benjamin

1731	1753	1789
born	builds a clock	sees eclipse that he predicted

14

In August 1791 Benjamin wrote

a letter to Thomas Jefferson.

Thomas was a slave owner.

Benjamin thought slavery

was wrong. He said Thomas

should help African-Americans.

Thomas made no promises.

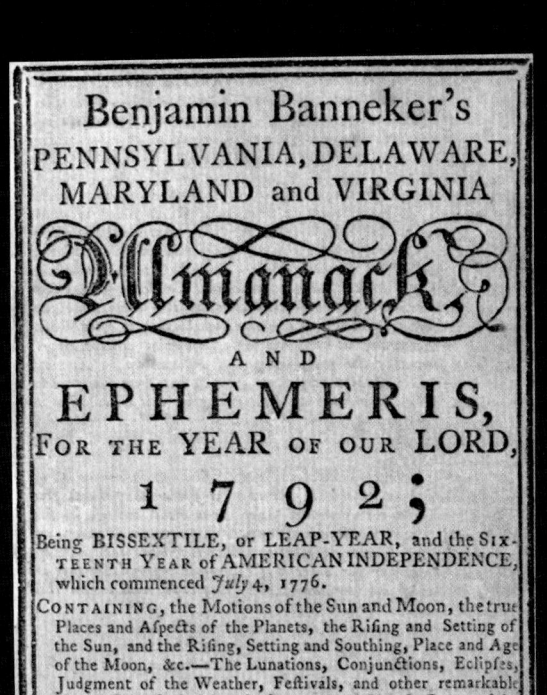

Benjamin Banneker's
PENNSYLVANIA, DELAWARE,
MARYLAND and VIRGINIA

Almanack

AND

EPHEMERIS,

FOR THE YEAR OF OUR LORD,

1 7 9 2;

Being BISSEXTILE, or LEAP-YEAR, and the SIX-
TEENTH YEAR of AMERICAN INDEPENDENCE,
which commenced *July* 4, 1776.

CONTAINING, the Motions of the Sun and Moon, the true
Places and Aspects of the Planets, the Rising and Setting of
the Sun, and the Rising, Setting and Southing, Place and Age
of the Moon, &c.—The Lunations, Conjunctions, Eclipses,
Judgment of the Weather, Festivals, and other remarkable
Days; Days for holding the Supreme and Circuit Courts of the
United States, as also the usual Courts in *Pennsylvania, Delaware, Maryland*, and *Virginia*.—ALso, several useful Tables,
and valuable Receipts.—Various Selections from the Com-
monplace-Book of the *Kentucky Philosopher*, an *American Sage*;
with interesting and entertaining Essays, in Prose and Verse—
the whole comprising a greater, more pleasing, and useful Va-
riety, than any Work of the *Kind* and *Price* in *North-America*.

BALTIMORE: Printed and Sold, Wholesale and Retail, by
WILLIAM GODDARD and JAMES ANGELL, at their Print-
ing-Office, in *Market-Street*.—Sold, also, by Mr. JOSEPH
CRUKSHANK, Printer, in *Market-Street*, and Mr. DANIEL
HUMPHREYS, Printer, in *South-Front-Street*, *Philadelphia*—
and by Messrs. HANSON and BOND, Printers, in *Alexandria*

1731
born

1753
builds a clock

1789
sees eclipse that
he predicted

Later in Life

Benjamin wanted to share his studies with the world. He wrote a book of helpful facts called an almanac. In 1792 his first almanac was published. Later he published five more.

1791

helps plan U.S. capital;
writes to Thomas Jefferson

1792

first almanac
is published

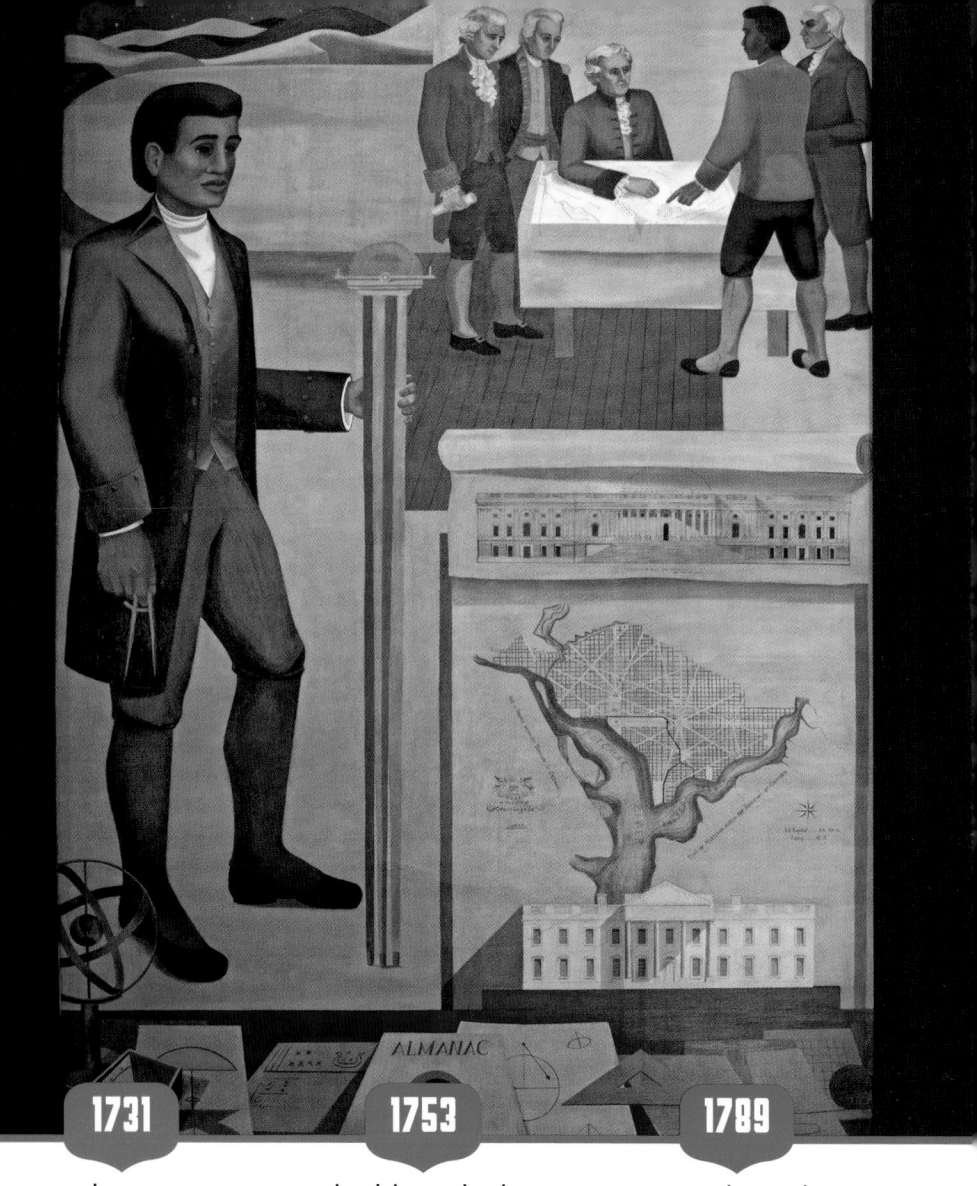

1731
born

1753
builds a clock

1789
sees eclipse that
he predicted

In Benjamin's time there were few well-known African-American thinkers. But Benjamin showed that African-Americans could invent things, write books, and plan whole cities.

1791

helps plan U.S. capital; writes to Thomas Jefferson

1792

first almanac is published

a postage stamp in Benjamin's honor

1731
born

1753
builds a clock

1789
sees eclipse that
he predicted

20

Benjamin died in 1806.
He is remembered for his
work and his almanacs.
Several schools and
museums are named
for Benjamin today.

1791	1792	1806
helps plan U.S. capital; writes to Thomas Jefferson	first almanac is published	dies

Glossary

almanac—a book published every year that has facts on many subjects, such as farming

astronomy—the study of stars, planets, and other objects in space

capital—the city in a country where the government is based

invent—to think up and make something new

predict—to say what you think will happen in the future

publish—to create a piece of writing and make it available to the public

scientist—a person who studies the world around us

slave—a person who is owned by another person

solar eclipse—a period of daytime darkness when the moon passes between the sun and Earth

Thomas Jefferson—the third president of the United States; Jefferson was secretary of state when Benjamin wrote a letter to him

Read More

Carney, Elizabeth. *Planets.* National Geographic Readers. Washington, D.C.: National Geographic, 2012.

James, Lincoln. *Solar Eclipses.* Science Scope. New York: PowerKids Press, 2009.

Kalman, Maira. *Thomas Jefferson: Life, Liberty and the Pursuit of Everything.* New York: Nancy Paulsen Books, 2014.

Internet Sites

FactHound offers a safe, fun way to find Internet sites related to this book. All of the sites on FactHound have been researched by our staff.

Here's all you do:
Visit *www.facthound.com*
Type in this code: 9781491405000

Check out projects, games and lots more at
www.capstonekids.com

Critical Thinking Using the Common Core

1. How did Benjamin Banneker help create Washington, D.C.? (Key Ideas and Details)

2. Look at the picture on page 8. How was Benjamin's clock different from the clocks we use today? (Integration of Knowledge and Ideas)

Index

almanacs, 17, 21
astronomy, 11
birth, 5
city planner, 13, 19
clock, 9
death, 21
family, 5, 7
inventor, 9, 19

Jefferson, Thomas, 15
Maryland, 5
schooling, 7
scientist, 5, 11
slavery, 5, 15
solar eclipse, 11
Washington, D.C., 13
writer, 5, 17, 19

Word Count: 232
Grade: 1
Early-Intervention Level: 21